I0169670

The King Who Befriends

Authority That Draws You Close

Bonnie Jean Schaefer

Dream Doers Publishing LLC

Copyright © 2025 by Dream Doers Publishing LLC

All rights reserved.

Published by Dream Doers Publishing LLC
Tobaccoville, North Carolina

Unless otherwise noted, all Scripture quotations are taken from the Christian Standard Bible®, Copyright © 2017 by Holman Bible Publishers. Used by permission. Christian Standard Bible® and CSB® are federally registered trademarks of Holman Bible Publishers. Pronouns referring to God have been capitalized for emphasis.

No portion of this book may be reproduced in any form without written permission from the publisher or author, except as permitted by U.S. copyright law.

Book Cover by Bonnie Jean Schaefer

Paperback ISBN: 978-0-9907463-8-6

CONTENTS

WHY THIS BOOK EXISTS

Since I accepted Christ as my Savior at age four, grew up in a Christian home, and spent my college years earning a Bible degree, I know what I believe theologically.

But a few years ago, I wanted something more personal, more relational, more memorable. I wanted to distill everything I'd learned from Scripture into a framework that felt like a story rather than systematic theology. Because God's roles are intentional and tell a story of creation, redemption, and sanctification.

This book thus tells the story of God's relationship with humanity through seven essential roles: Creator, King, Judge, Savior, Father, Friend, and Helper. It's not meant to be comprehensive study of God's character, but it is an exploration of how we get to relate to Him daily, personally, intimately.

I wanted to strip away the fluff and get straight to the heart of who God is and how I can relate to Him moment by moment.

Why I Write Like I'm Talking to God

This isn't a typical theology book because I didn't want to teach about God. I wanted to talk to God about who He is. That's simply how I process truth. When I journal, when I pray, when I wrestle with profound questions, I talk them through with Him.

We can approach God just like we approach the people we love most. We should be curious about who He is, eager to discover new depths of His character. So instead of writing academic explanations, I wrote conversations. Instead of systematic arguments, I wrote prayers.

So listen in on my talks with God about His roles in my life because this book is designed to be a catalyst for your prayers, a launching pad for deeper exploration of who God is and how He relates specifically to you.

To be clear, this book is for Christians — new or seasoned — who want to move from knowing about God to knowing God personally. If you're exploring faith for the first time, start with the "Answer the King" section at the end before reading the chapters.

How to Experience This Book

Each chapter unfolds as a prayer — an authentic conversation with God about one of His roles in my life. You're not just reading theology; you're overhearing someone wrestling with, wondering about, and worshipping the God who reveals Himself as "I AM."

Read it slowly. These aren't quick devotional snippets. Each chapter explores profound truths about God's character that deserve time to penetrate your heart and mind.

Read it prayerfully. Since every chapter is written as prayer, consider making it your own conversation with God. Let my words spark your words. Let my questions ignite your questions. Let my worship inspire your worship.

Read it personally. While I write from my experience, insert your own story. Make these conversations between you and God about who He is and what that means for your unique life.

My Heart for You

I simply want to know God. And I want everyone who reads this book to know God in the context of a relationship, not mere facts.

My prayer is that these conversations don't merely inform you about God's roles but draw you into experiencing those roles personally. I pray that you discover what I'm still discovering: instead of God's absolute authority being something to fear, it's the bedrock for the most secure, intimate relationship imaginable.

When you truly encounter the King who befriends, you'll discover that His power and His love aren't competing forces. Rather, His authority IS His love in action.

Let the conversation begin.

Opening Prayer

Father,

Who are You in relation to me? And why does who You are matter to me?

You play many roles in my life, and I will never begin to comprehend them all or how magnificent You are this side of eternity. But You do make Yourself known to me in ways I can understand well enough to have a deep, meaningful relationship with You.

You have shown me seven key roles You hold and how I relate to You as a result:

You are my Creator. I am the created.

You are my King. I am subject to Your authority.

You are my Judge. I am accountable to You.

You are my Savior. I am Your servant.

You are my Father. I am Your child.

You are my Friend. I walk with You.

You are my Helper. You live in me.

Among other attributes, these roles demonstrate Your power, Your love, Your compassion, Your perfection, Your righteousness, Your leadership, and Your expectations. You love me and want me to draw close to You.

Your attributes and characteristics remain constant. You are faithful, ever-present, loving, gracious, merciful, just, holy, righteous, honest, and all-powerful. You are God. The only God. The almighty. The everlasting. The King of kings and Lord of lords.

In short, You reveal that knowing You as King doesn't distance me from You. It brings me closer.

Because You are the King who befriends Your people.
In Christ,
Amen

1

— • —

CREATOR

THE FOUNDATION

FATHER,

You exist. You spoke the world into existence. From nothing!

But I didn't understand what that meant until I sat in a tenth-grade biology classroom listening to my teacher talk about evolution. She spoke with certainty about the origin of humanity across millions of years — apes to humans, chance devoid of purpose, survival of the fittest.

She sounded confident. I felt confused.

I knew she was wrong, but I didn't know why it mattered.

What difference does it make where we came from? We're here now, experiencing life as sinners in need of a Savior. Why does it matter whether man came from You or an ape?

I'd known You as my Creator since I was four. "In the beginning God created the heavens and the earth" (Genesis 1:1). The easiest verse I ever memorized. Simple. True.

But I didn't realize I needed to dig deeper until years later as a freshman in college.

In an earth-science class taught from a Christian worldview, my professor showed an image on the screen. One built on God's Word. One built on man's ideas.

And suddenly, I saw it.

By attacking the foundation of our origin, everything else crumbles. If You're not the Creator, the Bible falls apart. The rest of the story can't be true.

No God, no Designer. No Designer, no meaning. No meaning, no morals. No morals, no rules.

By rejecting You as Creator, the world gave itself permission to live without You.

I had to choose: believe the theory of evolution or believe the Bible. So I examined the evidence.

Evidence Everywhere

When I walk along the shoreline, I feel sand between my toes, hear the waves crash onto the shore, and watch the tide ebb and flow.

I climb mountains and stare at ranges that stretch beyond vision, valleys carved by forces I can't fathom.

I watch seasons cycle from winter's death to spring's resurrection, summer's warmth to fall's beauty, then back to dormancy before life breaks through again. I see veins on leaves matching veins beneath my skin.

Spiders weave intricate webs. Birds compose songs. Trees grow deeper roots to reach greater heights.

I don't need a super intellect or an advanced degree to see Your fingerprints. In me. In others. In nature. In the breath I take and the gravity that holds me.

Design declares a Designer.

Beauty reveals intention.

Order proves authority.

Everything in creation is visible evidence of the invisible God. The universe keeps shouting the same truth: You exist.

The Designer Who Knows My Name

"So God created man in His own image; He created him in the image of God; He created them male and female" (Genesis 1:27).

You didn't mass-produce humanity. You intentionally design every human being. From the wealthiest entrepreneur to the poorest tribal member in the most remote village, we're all made on purpose by You, in Your image, for Your glory.

You weave people together with talents and gifts before we are even born. Then You see us through from birth to death, wanting us to spend our lives fellowshipping with You, worshipping You, glorifying You with the gifts You've given.

"For it was You who created my inward parts; You knit me together in my mother's womb. I will praise You because I have been remarkably and wondrously made. Your works are wondrous, and I know this very well" (Psalm 139:13–14).

You designed me specifically when you made me creative, strategic, athletic, and just quirky enough to be my own brand of weird. In my weirdness, I spent my childhood lost in imaginary worlds, creating characters from thin air, lying in bed dreaming about possibilities. You gave me a wild imagination to dream, reason to think in systems, and a quiet drive to stretch my physical limits through running.

I am alive because You wanted me to exist. I bear Your fingerprints. I was made to reveal You.

When I write stories, I echo Your creativity.

When I solve problems, I reflect Your wisdom.

When I love others, I mirror Your heart.

You made me to show the world what You are like.

That's my purpose — to glorify You. That alone makes me valuable.

My value thus doesn't come from wealth or achievements or looks or trinkets or social status. It comes from You, my Creator. Because You made me in Your image.

Being made in Your image doesn't mean I look like You. It means I reflect Your character and that I was created with the capacity and desire for relationship, just as You exist in perfect unity.

The Trinity is a model of complete harmony, and in reflecting that, I long for connection — with You and with the people You have placed in my life to love, encourage, and connect with. Furthermore, You desire relationship with us, and in that invitation, You provide the sense of belonging our hearts crave.

Yet You don't force any relationship with Yourself on me. Instead, You present me with the opportunity to choose. Your decision to create me came hand-in-hand with the gift of choice — whether I will serve You or not.

You didn't preselect who would choose You; rather, You offer salvation to all, graciously invite every person to choose You, and through Your Spirit You give us the understanding and strength to respond in faith.

The ability to choose is what makes love genuine. Because love requires freedom.

Creating us was risky. You knew we would rebel, and You knew it would break Your heart when we rebelled. Still You gave me freedom, knowing I would use it to walk away.

What I can never walk away from is the fact that You made me. Sin distorts but never deletes Your image in me. It breaks fellowship, not identity. Every person still carries eternal worth because we were formed by eternal hands.

My value remains constant despite my circumstances. That's why rich and poor, famous and unknown, tall and short, light skinned and dark skinned and every shade in between all have the same value. We share the same source and sustainer of life: YOU.

The Source and Sustainer of Life

Because You sustain what You made, Your care is continuous, active, personal. You value what you created enough care for the sparrow and for me.

You didn't create the universe only to ignore it. Day after day, You uphold the orbit of the planets and the heart beating in my chest.

I've seen what happens to abandoned houses. They are overtaken by vines. Paint fades. Roofs collapse. Walls decay. Without the care of a homeowner, the house becomes uninhabitable. The same would happen to this world without Your sustaining power. Chaos would prevail, and I would cease to exist.

Thank You for being present even when I ignore You.

Thank You for caring for me even when I take You for granted.

Thank You for making me and claiming me as Your own.

"Acknowledge that the Lord is God. He made us, and we are His — His people, the sheep of His pasture" (Psalm 100:3).

You made me. I belong to You.

When I forget that, I chase empty goals and wonder why they don't satisfy. But when I remember You're the Creator, everything aligns. Meaning returns. Purpose drives my actions.

Because You created me, You define me.

Because You define me, You direct me.

You designed me on purpose for Your pleasure.

You are the reason I exist and the reason I endure.

You are the Creator and Sustainer of my soul.

Understanding who You are as my Creator gives meaning to my life, yet our connection extends further. As I come to know You as my King, that relationship grows even deeper.

2

— • —

KING

THE AUTHORITY

FATHER,

I have always known You as my Creator. That truth has been a part of me for as long as I can remember. Yet, for most of my life, I never connected Your role as Creator to Your authority over me. Only in recent years did I begin to understand that relationship more deeply.

I recall a moment when I asked You a simple yet profound question: "Why do You get to make the rules?"

It was then that the answer became clear. If You made me, then You have the right to rule me. And if You rule me, it means I do not set my own rules for life. Your authority comes from the fact that You created me.

Because when you create something, you have authority over it.

That realization dismantled my illusion of control. It was both terrifying and freeing.

When I write novels, my characters live in the world I design. They move, speak, and make choices, but always within the story I imagined. They can't act outside of the established world rules or the story will lose credibility and crumble. They also don't rewrite my plot. They exist because I imagined them to life.

And that's how I began to understand You.

You are the Author of existence. You spoke creation into being. You set the laws of life and love. You decide what's right, what's true, what's real.

"The Lord has established His throne in heaven, and His kingdom rules over all" (Psalm 103:19).

Your throne wasn't inherited or voted upon because it's rooted in creation itself. You rule because You made the world. You own everything because You spoke everything into existence.

Earthly kings borrow power. They rise and fall. They are limited by time and weakness. But You as the eternal King answer to no one. You cannot be corrupted, defeated, or replaced. You are wise, holy, and just. Everything You do is motivated by love.

"Our God is in heaven and does whatever He pleases" (Psalm 115:3).

You are the King of kings. Your kingdom has no end.

And somehow, You invite me to live under Your rule. If You truly rule everything, then every decision I make either honors or resists Your reign.

The King Who Rules Well

You don't govern out of pride or distance. You rule with design. You know how life works because You made life itself.

Your laws aren't burdens. They're blueprints. They're the framework for peace, joy, and order.

Like a coach who sets boundaries so the team can win or parents who teach rules so their kids can thrive, Your commands are love expressed through structure.

"For this is what love for God is: to keep His commands. And His commands are not a burden" (1 John 5:3).

When I ignore the physical, relational, or spiritual laws You built into the world, life starts to fall apart.

- **Physical law:** Ignore rest and health breaks down.

- **Relational law:** Betray trust and hearts fracture.

- **Spiritual law:** Reject You and the soul starves.

Your ways aren't restrictions; they're reality. They aren't control; they're compassion.

The boundaries You set are guardrails designed to protect me from dangers I don't even know are lurking in the dark. They keep me from plunging off cliffs I can't see in time.

You know I need those boundaries, even when I resist them. Because You know what I'm made for.

Every time I've chosen to obey You, peace has followed. Every time I've trusted Your command, even when it was hard, the outcome has proved You right. Your rules lead to life and joy and peace.

The Law of the King

Your authority is moral, not arbitrary. You rule through truth that reflects Your character. You have written that truth on every human heart.

Even those who deny You still sense it.

We *ought* to tell the truth. We *ought* to protect life. We *ought* to respect others and live with kindness. That inward sense of right and wrong comes from You. It's the echo of Your voice in the conscience of every person.

You are the Lawgiver who defines righteousness.

Because You are holy, Your moral law is holy. Because You are good, Your commandments are good. And when we break them, it is not just rebellion against a rule. It is rebellion against You.

Earthly law must submit to Yours, and I must submit to those laws unless they contradict the greater commands You have spoken and revealed to me in Your word.

When nations write laws against murder or theft, they are tracing the lines of Your design. When governments pursue justice, they mirror the Judge they were made to reflect.

That's why justice must exist. Because right and wrong are real. Because sin is an offense against the King Himself. You don't shift Your standards with culture; Your law stands as steady as Your throne.

To obey You is to be free.

The Paradox of Freedom

Submission equals freedom? That doesn't make sense.

Everything in me wants independence to make my own choices, chase my own dreams, do things my way.

But the more I try to rule myself, the more enslaved I become to sin, Satan, and self.

I thought indulgence was freedom — eat what I want, when I want, as much as I want. But indulgence only trapped me in craving.

I thought independence was freedom, but it just left me carrying burdens I couldn't lift.

True freedom lives inside surrender.

When I submit to You, I stop fighting gravity. I stop denying design. I start to breathe again.

"Your word is a lamp for my feet and a light on my path" (Psalm 119:105).

You could have made obedience automatic, forced, robotic. But You didn't. You gave choice. Because love without freedom isn't love.

You want willing hearts, not programmed servants. You are a King who makes Himself vulnerable to rejection for the sake of relationship.

The Problem With My Rebellion

Still, I rebel.

I want to be queen of my own life, ruler of my own heart. The world cheers me on.

"Follow your truth."

"Be your own boss."

"Believe in yourself."

But those are lies wrapped in glitter.

I'm not omniscient. I'm not omnipotent. I'm not holy. I'm not You.

Rejecting You doesn't make me free; it just trades masters. Appetite rules. Fear rules. Idols rule. Something always does.

When I reject You, I step outside my own design. Like a fish gasping on dry land, I can't survive outside the water of Your will.

This is why our world seems so disordered. Everyone wants to be in charge. People battle for power that isn't truly theirs.

Pride blinds me to the truth: autonomy is an illusion.

I'm always serving someone.

Better to serve the good and perfect King than the cruel tyrants of sin and self.

My rebellion doesn't dethrone You. It just breaks me.

"For all have sinned and fall short of the glory of God" (Romans 3:23).

You are holy. I am not. You deserve perfect obedience. I give imperfect submission. You made me for relationship, yet my sin creates distance.

And in that distance, I feel the ache of treason.

The King who made me, who loves me, who rules with justice...I've rebelled against Him.

Forgive me for the times I've treated Your law like suggestion instead of truth. Teach me to love obedience as worship.

The Just King

You cannot ignore sin and remain good. You cannot excuse rebellion and still be righteous.

Because You are holy, justice isn't optional. It's essential.

The authority of the King who establishes the law cannot be separated from the responsibility to uphold it. The One who defines what is righteous must also be the One who judges unrighteousness. The very throne that governs must also hold accountable those who transgress.

Your holiness demands this unwavering commitment to justice, and Your love affirms it.

It is at the intersection of these roles — King and Judge, sovereign and standard-bearer — that the need to address sin becomes clear. Because You are both holy and loving, You must deal with sin.

A King without judgment is a figurehead, not a ruler. Laws without enforcement are suggestions, not standards. If You establish what is right, You must also address what is wrong.

Authority without accountability collapses into chaos.

That's why the King who rules must also be the Judge who holds His subjects accountable.

3

JUDGE

THE VERDICT

FATHER,

You are my Creator who made everything, who owns me, who longs for a relationship with me.

You are my King who establishes the rules of Your kingdom from the placement of the stars to the pull of gravity to the moral laws that teach me how to love You and others.

Since You are the King, You must also be Judge.

Because what good is a King who is incapable of holding His subjects accountable?

What good is a kingdom if wrong is never made right?

What good are laws if rebellion carries no consequence?

So You embrace the role of Judge. A judge evaluates evidence, interprets law, and delivers an impartial decision.

As Judge, You weigh my actions, thoughts, and motives against Your holy standard. You interpret Your law with flawless understanding because You wrote it. You deliver verdicts that hold justice and mercy together because You are both holy and loving.

You are constantly holding me accountable to Your commands as revealed in Your Word, but You don't always administer justice in the moment. Sometimes You choose to wait to give me time to repent and return. Sometimes You take action right away the way You did with Adam and Eve.

Adam's Judgement Becomes Mine

When Adam and Eve disobeyed Your command to not eat of the Tree of Knowledge of Good and Evil, You stepped into the role of Judge and administered justice.

They left the garden; death entered the world. Separation from You became the new reality because holiness cannot coexist with sin.

You have never stopped being Judge, because the kingdom would collapse without justice. To ignore sin would deny Your own character. You judge because You are good.

But Adam's disobedience didn't just affect him and Eve. It affected me. It affected every human who would ever live. Because You didn't create Adam to act for himself alone. You appointed him to act on behalf of all humanity.

He was our representative. Our federal head. The one who stood in for the entire human race.

When a president signs a treaty, that decision binds the entire nation. When a team captain accepts the terms of a game, those rules apply to every player. The representative's choice becomes everyone's reality.

That's what happened in the garden.

Yes, Eve ate first. But You appointed Adam as the head, the one who carried authority and responsibility for humanity. When he chose to follow her into rebellion instead of leading her back to obedience, his choice carried the weight of representation. His sin — not hers — became the hinge point of history because he was the federal head You appointed to stand for all of us.

Adam stood before You as more than just an individual. He stood as mankind's representative. You gave him authority to choose on behalf of all his descendants. And when he chose rebellion, his choice became our inheritance.

"Therefore, just as sin entered the world through one man, and death through sin, in this way death spread to all people, because all sinned" (Romans 5:12).

Adam's sin didn't just set a bad example. It severed humanity's relationship with You. His spiritual death became mine. His guilt became mine. His separation from You became mine.

Born into Condemnation

I inherited my sin nature from Adam. Not because I personally ate the fruit, but because he ate it as my representative. His rebellion bound me to sin before I ever committed my first act of disobedience.

I sin because I am a sinner by nature. I was born spiritually dead. Separated from You. Alienated from my God.

This feels unfair until I realize You structured it this way for a reason. If one man's failure could condemn humanity, then one Man's obedience could save it. If Adam's choice could bind me to death, then another Representative's choice could free me for life.

And if I did nothing to earn my sin nature, I can do nothing to earn my salvation. But I must receive it. I must believe.

That's why You appointed Adam to act on my behalf. And when he failed, You made room for a new Representative. One who would succeed where Adam failed. One whose righteousness could cover my guilt the same way Adam's guilt covered me.

But I'm getting ahead of myself. Right now, I'm still standing in Adam's failure.

And nothing I do can mend that rift with You. Unclean people can't clean themselves.

"All of us have become like something unclean, and all our righteous acts are like a polluted garment; all of us wither like a leaf, and our iniquities carry us away like the wind" (Isaiah 64:6).

The earthly consequence for sin is death. But worse is the eternal consequence: eternity in hell, forever separated from You.

Your righteousness demands I pay these consequences. Your justice cannot overlook my rebellion. Your holiness cannot coexist with my sin. Your wrath against sin must be satisfied.

Before the Throne

So I stand in the throne room of Your justice now.

This isn't like family court my sisters and I once faced year after year as foster parents, with judges dressed in black robes deciding a child's fate.

You are nothing like those judges.

You don't sift partial evidence or second-hand reports. You see the whole story — every action, every thought, every motive.

You sit as my Creator who made me, as my King who rules me, and as my Judge who holds me accountable.

You know everything about me. I have no secrets from You. You know every thought, every motive, every selfish desire, every turn toward ease instead of obedience.

Choosing to overeat. Choosing to scroll instead of stewarding the work You gave. Choosing silence when love required a word. It is all sin.

I have no excuse. You know my heart. You know why I do what I do. There is no alibi when the Witness is everywhere and the Judge is all-wise.

Every small sin is not "small." It is treason scaled to the size of my opportunity. I have rejected Your authority.

And I inherited the inclination to reject You from Adam, my representative.

You ask, *What did you do with the gifts I gave? What did you do with My Word? What did you do with Me?*

You aren't weighing productivity or public good; You're looking at my heart. And I know that when I stand before You, I will not be able to stand at all.

Undone Before Holiness

When Isaiah saw You high and lifted up, he said, "Woe is me for I am ruined because I am a man of unclean lips and live among a people of unclean lips, and because my eyes have seen the King, the Lord of Armies" (Isaiah 6:5).

When Peter experienced Your power in a boat overflowing with fish, he recognized his own sinfulness. "When Simon Peter saw this, he fell at Jesus's knees and said, 'Go away from me, because I am a sinful man, Lord!'" (Luke 5:8).

When John beheld the glorified Christ on Patmos, he dropped to the ground before You as though dead. "When I saw Him, I fell at His feet like a dead man" (Revelation 1:17a).

These were Your servants, faithful men who loved You. One unveiled moment of Your holiness brought them to their knees.

What will it be like for me?

Your light pours through me like fire through paper. There is nowhere to hide a thought, nowhere to park an excuse. My practiced defenses dissolve. The unfiltered, unedited me stands in the center of Your gaze.

I sense the rip of every mask. Every minimizing phrase falls dead at my feet. Nothing to hide. Only what is true, laid bare before the God of truth.

The Weight of Justice

You see all the times I chose comfort over obedience, convenience over compassion, indulgence over discipline. Little sins, ordinary sins, the ones I excuse.

But You call every one rebellion.

Every "little" sin traces to this root rebellion. I wanted my way, not Yours.

My glory, not Yours. My rule, not Yours.

Each act of self-will is treason against the King who made me. And You cannot overlook them. You cannot call wrong right.

Your holiness demands consistency; Your love demands accountability.

And so the light presses heavier. It doesn't crush in anger; it crushes with truth. It feels like standing beneath the full reality of who You are: pure, clean, unbending.

Justice is not loud here; it is silent, steady, certain.

I fall to my knees.

The Standard I Cannot Meet

Your standard is holiness.

"For it is written, 'Be holy, because I am holy'" (1 Peter 1:16).

Perfect. Sinless. Pure.

I have fallen infinitely short.

Not "nearly made it." Catastrophically short. An infinite gap exists between Your holiness and my sin.

It's like offering You a penny when I owe trillions for my treason.

I cannot pay what I owe.

"Whoever keeps the entire law, and yet stumbles at one point, is guilty of breaking it all" (James 2:10).

This is not arithmetic where good cancels bad. The standard is perfection, and I am already fallen.

Maybe I can work harder? No. The standard is holiness, not improvement.

Maybe I can apologize and do better? No. The sin is already committed; future obedience does not erase past rebellion.

Maybe my good outweighs my bad? No. This is not a scale of averages but a standard of perfection.

Every door is locked. Every exit closed. Every hope extinguished.

I am out of options, out of excuses, out of air.

Condemned

The weight of my sin forces me lower until I'm on my face. Every defense dies in my throat.

"For the wages of sin is death" (Romans 6:23a).

Not only the death that ends breath, but the death that severs soul from You and lands me in hell. Hell is eternal torment, desperate desolation, separation from the You, the source of all good.

Hell is the full experience of separation from Your grace and the just expression of Your righteous judgment.

It holds No beauty because You are beauty. No love because You are love. No light because You are light.

And hell is justice for disobedience.

I am guilty.

You want me near You, yet You cannot pretend my guilt away. You will not lower Your standards. You cannot lower Your standards and still be good.

To let sin slide would make You unjust, and being unjust would mean that You would cease to be God.

But You are God, and You take no delight in this sentence. Your justice carries sorrow, not spite. You desire reconciliation, not ruin.

You judge because You love too deeply to let sin survive.

You pronounce guilt so that grace can be real.

The Desperate Cry

I am on my face before You, knowing there is nothing I can offer. Every breath a plea for mercy.

Like the tax collector in the temple, I cannot lift my eyes. I beat my breast and whisper through tears, "God, be merciful to me, a sinner."

I have no claim, no leverage, no bargain to strike.

I am a guilty rebel before a righteous Judge, with no defense and no hope.

I stand condemned.

I deserve hell.

There is nothing I can do.

I need Someone to pay the price for my sin.

I need a Savior.

And in that desperate moment, You stepped forward. Not to condemn me further, but to take my place.

4

SAVIOR

THE GREAT RESCUE

FATHER,

I collapsed before You as Judge.

Condemned. Guilty. The verdict was clear: I deserved punishment. Eternal separation. Hell. And there was nothing I could do to save myself.

I stood condemned in Adam. His failure as my representative bound me to sin and death. His choice in the garden became my inheritance. His rebellion became my nature.

But You didn't leave me there.

You appointed Adam to represent humanity, and when he failed, You made a way for a new Representative. One who would succeed where Adam failed. One whose obedience could cover my disobedience. One whose righteousness could become my righteousness.

You sent Christ to be my substitute, my Representative before the throne of justice.

"For just as through one man's disobedience the many were made sinners, so also through the one Man's obedience the many will be made righteous" (Romans 5:19).

Adam acted on my behalf and brought condemnation. Christ acted on my behalf and brought salvation.

Adam's choice bound me to death. Christ's choice freed me for life.

I deserved Your wrath, the righteous anger of a holy God against sin. But Christ absorbed that wrath in my place. He became my Representative, standing where Adam once stood, obeying where Adam disobeyed.

The God Who Pays What I Owe

There is a cost for my rebellion, and someone must pay it.

But in Your grace and mercy, that Someone doesn't have to be me.

So You sent Christ to pay my sin debt.

Why would You do that? How can the holy God love a rebel? How can the righteous Judge show mercy to someone who deserves condemnation?

"But God proves His own love for us in that while we were still sinners, Christ died for us" (Romans 5:8).

While I was still Your enemy, You rescued me.

You did so because You want to redeem me from my sin and restore me to fellowship with You. But Your holiness demands payment for my sin. Your wrath against sin must be appeased.

That payment is blood because blood represents life. And sin's penalty is a life taken.

Death means a life is forfeited. Blood is the visible evidence that life has been poured out.

"According to the law almost everything is purified with blood, and without the shedding of blood there is no forgiveness" (Hebrews 9:22).

But my sin taints my blood. I cannot offer my blood to pay the debt I owe because I'm not perfect. A contaminated sacrifice cannot pay for contamination.

I need a substitute. Someone perfect. Someone sinless. Someone who could die in my place and bear Your wrath instead of me.

Someone who could represent me without the stain of Adam's guilt.

But who could possibly qualify?

The God Who Becomes My Substitute

"The Word became flesh and dwelt among us. We observed His glory, the glory as the one and only Son from the Father, full of grace and truth" (John 1:14).

Jesus took the form of a man so He could sacrifice Himself for me. God became human. The infinite squeezed into the finite. The eternal entered time. The Creator became creation.

Why?

So You could die for me and bear the wrath I deserved.

Christ was born of a virgin, fully human yet without sin nature. He lived a perfect life as both fully man and fully God. For thirty-three years, He did what I could never do: He obeyed You perfectly.

And then He went to a cross.

"He made the One who did not know sin to be sin for us, so that in Him we might become the righteousness of God" (2 Corinthians 5:21).

On that cross, Jesus became sin. The sinless One took on my sin. The perfect Lamb bore my guilt. The righteous Judge poured out His wrath — the wrath I deserved — on Christ instead of me.

"Yet the Lord was pleased to crush Him severely. When You make Him a guilt offering, He will see His seed, He will prolong his days, and by His hand the Lord's pleasure will be accomplished" (Isaiah 53:10).

You crushed Your own Son so You wouldn't have to crush me. You punished Him so You could pardon me.

Christ offered His blood as payment for my sins. His perfect life satisfied Your justice. His innocent death paid my debt. Your holy anger at sin was fully expressed, completely satisfied, but it fell on Him, not me.

He didn't just pay my fine. He took the punishment I deserved for rebelling against God. He absorbed Your wrath. He stood under the full weight of Your judgment. He endured the hell I deserved.

I owe everything to what happened on that cross.

But the story doesn't end with death.

Victory in Christ

Three days later, You did what no one else has ever done or can ever do: You defeated death itself.

"For I passed on to you as most important what I also received: that Christ died for our sins according to the Scriptures, that He was buried, that he was raised on the third day according to the Scriptures" (1 Corinthians 15:3-4).

When Christ arose from the grave, He proved that death had no power over Him. Sin was conquered. Satan was defeated. Hell itself was robbed of its victory. Your wrath was satisfied. Your justice was served. Your love triumphed.

That's why Jesus is my Savior. He redeemed me from my sins. He set me free from my bond to sin and bonded me to You instead.

The transaction is complete. The debt is paid. The wrath is satisfied. The victory is won!

And all I have to do is believe.

"If you confess with your mouth, 'Jesus is Lord,' and believe in your heart that God raised him from the dead, you will be saved" (Romans 10:9).

I do believe, God. I have believed since I was four years old, when my mother knelt beside me and prayed with me while I confessed Christ as my Lord and asked You to forgive my sins.

That moment when I believed, You saved my soul from the *penalty* of sin — eternal damnation —because of the blood of Christ.

"Therefore, if anyone is in Christ, he is a new creation; the old has passed away, and see, the new has come!" (2 Corinthians 5:17).

My salvation is secure and can never be repealed. I didn't earn it, so I can't lose it. It depends on Your work, not mine. Your promise, not my performance.

"I give them eternal life, and they will never perish. No one will snatch them out of My hand" (John 10:28).

But salvation isn't just a one-time event. Every day, Your Spirit works in me to make me more like Christ. So you continue to save me from the *power* of sin into holiness.

When I meet You in glory, You will complete the work by saving me from the *presence* of sin forever. No more struggle. No more temptation. No more war between flesh and spirit.

I will be perfectly holy, just as You are holy.

"Dear friends, we are God's children now, and what we will be has not yet been revealed. We know that when He appears, we will be like Him because we will see Him as He is" (1 John 3:2).

From Enemy to Daughter

When I stood before You as Judge, I was condemned. But Christ took my place. He absorbed Your wrath. He bore the punishment.

"God presented him as an atoning sacrifice in His blood, received through faith, to demonstrate His righteousness, because in His restraint God passed over the sins previously committed" (Romans 3:25).

Christ didn't just pay a debt. He satisfied Your righteous anger. And the verdict changed: Not guilty. Forgiven. Justified. Declared righteous.

"Therefore, there is now no condemnation for those in Christ Jesus" (Romans 8:1).

I was Your enemy. Now I'm Your child.

I was under Your wrath. Now I'm under Your grace.

I was condemned by Your law. Now I'm covered by Your love.

You didn't just save me FROM something. You saved me TO something. To relationship. To purpose. To eternal life with You as Your daughter.

What does it mean that You're not just my Creator and King and Judge and Savior, but that You've adopted me as Your child?

What does it mean to call the Savior who rescued me my Father?

5

FATHER

THE ADOPTION

FATHER,

The Savior who bore my wrath now calls me His child. The throne room of justice has become the living room of family.

"And because you are sons, God sent the Spirit of his Son into our hearts, crying, 'Abba, Father!'" (Galatians 4:6).

Abba is the cry of a heart that knows it belongs.

Sin once separated me from You. Though You were already my Creator and King and Judge, rebellion blocked me from the rights of Your family. But You loved me so much that You sent Your Son to bear my punishment, to pay the price I could never pay. When I chose Christ, You legally and eternally adopted me into Your family.

I am Yours twice over — created and adopted. And You gave me a new name. I went from Bonnie IN ADAM Jean Schaefer to Bonnie **IN CHRIST** Jean Schaefer. My identity is forever sealed IN CHRIST.

But what does it mean that You are my Father?

The Model of Fatherhood

A true father protects, provides, teaches, and nurtures his children. He ensures their safety, meets their needs, imparts wisdom, and encourages their growth. His discipline is grounded in love, and he fights fiercely on behalf of his children. I have witnessed these qualities firsthand in my own earthly dad. He is a living example of both strength and tenderness, embodying the characteristics of a faithful father.

My mother has modeled Your faithfulness in different but equally powerful ways. She has been steady when life shook, generous when resources were thin, and present through every season of my life. She taught me that love shows up, that faithfulness endures, and that Your character can be seen in quiet, consistent devotion.

But not everyone knows that kind of parenting. The kids my sisters and I fostered and eventually adopted came into our home because their parents failed them through abandonment or addiction. Yet You promise, "Even if my father and mother abandon me, the Lord cares for me" (Psalm 27:10).

No matter someone's earthly experience, anyone who chooses Christ receives the same perfect Father: faithful, loving, and secure.

You wanted me to be part of Your family so badly that You paid the ultimate price. You sacrificed Your Son — trading Christ's life for mine — so You could welcome me home.

In the moment I chose to accept Christ as my Savior, I went from spiritual orphan to spiritual heir. From outsider to daughter. You saw me lost and made me Yours.

Now when You look at me, You see Christ. Not my sin, but His righteousness.

Family Privileges

As Your child, I carry a new identity — free, forgiven, secure. Everything Christ has as Your Son, You share with me.

You care for all my needs: physical, emotional, spiritual. You bless beyond what I deserve. "If you then, who are evil, know how to give good gifts to your children, how much more will your Father in heaven give good things to those who ask him" (Matthew 7:11).

I see Your fingerprints everywhere — talents, opportunities, vision. You gave me a mind that loves to write stories, build systems, and teach truth. You shape me to reflect Your character through creativity and discipline.

"Blessed is the God and Father of our Lord Jesus Christ, who has blessed with every spiritual blessing in the heavens in Christ" (Ephesians 1:3).

Access when I pray. Peace when life shakes. Wisdom when I ask. The Spirit who empowers. These are family privileges, not wages I earn. They flow from belonging. And one way I know I belong is because you make Your expectations for my behavior clear.

Authority That Creates Safety

Every family has rules. Yours exist not for control, but for love. Because I know You, You hold me to higher standards.

Your discipline isn't punishment for paid-for sin; it's protection that corrects and trains me. Until I became a foster parent, I didn't fully understand this.

When our oldest foster daughter arrived at age three, she struggled with boundaries like set mealtimes and bedtimes. But soon those routines brought peace. They told her she was safe.

That's what Your authority does for me. Your boundaries are security, not restriction. "The boundary lines have fallen for me in pleasant places; indeed, I have a beautiful inheritance" (Psalm 16:6).

When I disobey, You correct me, not to cast me out but to call me back. Pardon ended my guilt once for all; fatherly forgiveness restores closeness every time I return.

Present in Every Storm

Still, You don't always spare me from pain. Christians still face disease, loss, and disaster. Not because You're powerless but because sin broke the world.

"For we know that the whole creation has been groaning together with labor pains until now" (Romans 8:22).

You promise presence, not ease. You didn't save Daniel from the lions' den; You joined him there. You didn't keep Shadrach from the fire; You walked in the flames with him. You don't always stop storms, but You steady me inside them.

Like when those dogs attacked my mini-goldendoodle. No one heard my cries for help as I shielded him with my body and fought to dislodge their teeth from his flesh. No one, that is, but You.

You kept those dogs from ripping me to shreds and later healed my tattered pup.

"I will be with you when you pass through the waters, and when you pass through the rivers, they will not overwhelm you. You will not be scorched when you walk through the fire, and the flame will not burn you" (Isaiah 43:2).

Your love refines, Your purpose redeems, Your presence comforts. With You as my Father, I am never alone.

Certain Hope for an Uncertain World

As my Father, You give me certain hope, alive and unshakable.

"Blessed be the God and Father of our Lord Jesus Christ. Because of His great mercy He has given us new birth into a living hope through the resurrection of Jesus Christ from the dead and into an inheritance that is imperishable, undefiled, and unfading, kept in heaven for you" (1 Peter 1:3-4).

Because Christ lives, hope lives. Hope for today. Hope for tomorrow. Hope for eternity. Certain hope.

That hope gets me up when despair whispers. It fuels faith when the world mocks obedience. Because I know the end of the story. The Father wins. Your children win.

But certain victory doesn't mean I get to forget You and do what I want because my eternal hope is secure. I am still responsible for obeying You today, and you discipline me when I get off track.

Because this life is training for eternity. Discipline shapes character; obedience builds strength.

"No discipline seems enjoyable at the time, but painful. Later on, however, it yields the peaceful fruit of righteousness to those who have been trained by it" (Hebrews 12:11).

You challenge me because You love me. You prune complacency. You push me to grow. You reveal weaknesses so I rely on You and the family You've placed me in.

"Now as we have many parts in one body, and all the parts do not have the same function, in the same way we who are many are one body in Christ and individually members of one another" (Romans 12:4-5).

You've made me a writer, leader, and athlete. When I use those gifts for Your glory, I feel Your pleasure. You delight in me because I'm Yours.

Thank You for designing me with purpose. Help me live boldly, write faithfully, and lead humbly so others meet their Father through my story.

The Father's Heart

You know what I need before I ask. You listen when I cry. You celebrate when I trust. You restore when I fail. You are patient, attentive, and faithful.

That belonging comes with forgiveness. You forgive fully and freely. As Judge, You pardoned me once for all. As Father, You forgive me daily. That's why I can forgive others. You wiped my slate clean; I can't hold debts against anyone else.

Your forgiveness gives peace. It restores fellowship and makes room for joy.

Thank You for adopting me, for never letting go, for loving me through growing pains and celebrating with me in joy.

You're my Father. My Abba. My Protector and Provider. You've given me gifts and dreams that reach beyond my lifetime.

And one of those gifts is friendship with Christ.

6

FRIEND

THE COMPANION

FATHER,

Every time I consider another way You relate to me, I feel You drawing closer. I see a progression in depth and intimacy from Creator to King, from King to Savior, from Savior to Father. And now from Father to Friend.

But this leap feels different.

Father is a defined role. You're clearly in charge. You make the rules, provide for me, protect me, correct me, and love me unconditionally. There's order and structure. You're above me, and I obey.

But Friend? That's different. Friendship feels side by side, like equals and companions. It requires vulnerability. And that's what I've avoided most.

I learned early that getting close could hurt. My best friend in high school vanished from my life without warning. One day she was there; the next, she wasn't. When she came back, she was different, and the bond was broken. I built walls after that, walls to keep me from being hurt again.

But You've shown me that friendship doesn't always end in loss. My mother proved that. The woman who knelt beside me when I was four and led me to You has become one of my closest friends in my adult life. She's taught me that true friendship weathers seasons, that love doesn't abandon, and that showing up is its own form of faithfulness. In her steady presence, I've learned what it means to be a friend who stays.

Nevertheless, I've kept a kind of distance in my relationship with You, I've kept a kind of distance. I can obey. I can serve. But friendship means opening my heart. And that feels scary.

Running has become my rhythm of reflection, the place where I wrestle with these walls. Every run starts the same: lacing shoes, stretching, feeling the hesitation in my muscles before I move. Just like my hesitations with You. It's easier to stay where I am than to start the run that might stretch me.

But Your role of Friend is clear and sure: "I do not call you servants anymore, because a servant doesn't know what his master is doing. I have called you friends, because I have made known to you everything I have heard from My Father" (John 15:15).

Servants follow orders. Friends know why. You invite me to move from duty to understanding, from running alone to running with You.

But how can I be friends with Someone who has all authority over me? You're the Creator. I'm the created. You're the King. I'm the subject. And yet, You humble Yourself to match my stride.

Like my running friend from church who slows her pace so I can keep up, You adjust to meet me where I am. You don't need to, but You choose to. You coach me as we go. You encourage when I lag. You challenge me when I coast.

That's what friendship looks like. You don't lose authority when You run beside me; You reveal it through humility.

Philippians 2:5-8 describes how You, the Son of God, "emptied" Yourself:

"Adopt the same attitude as that of Christ Jesus, who, existing in the form of God, did not consider equality with God as something to be exploited. Instead, He emptied Himself by assuming the form of a servant, taking on the likeness of humanity. And when He had come as a man, He humbled Himself by becoming obedient — even to death on a cross."

You slowed Your divine pace to match human steps.

You do that for me every day. You set the pace, but You never run so fast that I lose sight of You.

The Heart of a Running Friend

It's on my long runs where I talk to You more honestly than anywhere else. It starts with the rhythm of breath and footsteps. Before long, I'm telling You things I don't say out loud anywhere else.

You already know every thought before it forms: "Before a word is on my tongue, You know all about it, Lord" (Psalm 139:4).

But You still listen.

And as I speak, You speak back. Not with words I hear, but with thoughts that align with truth, with conviction that cuts through fear, with peace that settles into my chest. The longer I run, the more I feel the companionship. It's like You're beside me, not as my coach barking orders but as my Friend sharing the journey.

You let me see the why behind the what.

When I write, You show me the heart behind the stories. When I parent the kids we adopted, You show me the heart behind compassion. When I lead, You teach me to serve. These aren't assignments anymore. They're shared missions. Servants follow commands; friends share purpose.

Still, there are days I don't feel like running. Days when I question whether it's worth it, when I'm sore, tired, or discouraged. That's when You challenge me the most.

"You are my friends if you do what I command you" (John 15:14).

At first, that verse confused me. It sounded conditional. But obedience is the bond of friendship. I obey because I trust You. I trust because You've proven faithful.

You challenge me like my running buddy does when she says, "Just one more mile." She knows I can go farther than I think I can. You know the same about me. So You keep stretching me, teaching endurance in body and in faith.

Overwhelming Loneliness

When I started college, You were the only One I knew.

I showed up to softball tryouts and made the team as a walk-on. I gained teammates, but none of them were friends at first. Practices, classes, dorm life. I moved through them like a ghost.

I had never felt so lonely as I did that first month away from home.

I felt an ache in my soul for connection. But at the end of practice one fall afternoon, when the dark void of loneliness was about to consume me, my coach reminded us that You are a God who longs to enjoy a relationship with us.

I imagined You waiting at the end of that field, arms open, ready to listen, ready to run beside me. I felt Your presence in that moment: Your arms around my soul, Your companionship filling the loneliness.

"The Lord is near the brokenhearted; He saves those crushed in spirit" (Psalm 34:18).

That memory anchors me. You showed up when I felt unseen. You became the Friend who never leaves mid-race.

And I became friends with people on that softball team who I'm still friends with today.

Even now, there are days when I don't feel You near. I pray, and it feels like silence. Yet I've learned that friendship isn't built on feelings. It's built on trust.

David knew that, too. He cried out in a prophetic way, "My God, my God, why have you abandoned me? Why are You so far from my deliverance and from my words of groaning?" (Psalm 22:1).

But David kept talking. Kept running. Kept trusting.

That's what You ask of me. To keep running beside You, even when the air feels heavy and the silence stretches. To trust that You're still there, setting the pace I can't yet see.

"Trust in the Lord with all your heart, and do not rely on your own understanding" (Proverbs 3:5).

Trusting the Lead

A few years ago, I had an opportunity to trust one of those lifelong friends from the college softball team when she invited me on a backpacking trip in Chile. I'd only been backpacking twice before, but she had dozens of trips under her belt.

So I followed her lead. She planned the route, carried extra gear, and guided me through rough terrain.

We saw amazing views and hiked challenging paths because I trusted her to lead. I never could have completed that eight-day hike on my own.

As my Friend, You are my Guide through life. You see the trail from start to finish while I only see the next turn. You ask me to trust Your route even when I can't see the destination.

And You keep asking for my heart. Not just obedience. Not just service. My heart.

Servants give effort. Friends give affection. You've given me all of You; You want all of me in return.

"Casting all your cares on Him, because He cares about you" (1 Peter 5:7).

So I tell You my fears — the doubts about dreams, the struggles with raising these adopted kids, the temptation to quit when the trail gets tough. You listen because honesty builds intimacy, not because You need information.

You've proven that friendship with You is safe. You don't weaponize my weakness. You don't run off when the pace slows. You stay beside me.

Learning from the Friend I've Found

Your friendship is teaching me how to be a better friend to others.

"Iron sharpens iron, and one person sharpens another" (Proverbs 27:17).

I'm learning to slow my pace for others, to encourage without controlling, to be present without fixing. You model patience with me, so I can offer patience to them.

"We love because He first loved us" (1 John 4:19).

Your friendship gives me courage to risk connection again, to open up to people, to trust that love doesn't always end in loss.

The Finish Line of Friendship

It never ceases to amaze me that You, the King of the universe, would choose to be my Friend. You willingly match Your stride to mine, walking at my pace. This isn't out of need, for You lack nothing; instead, You desire companionship with me. You created me for this kind of fellowship so I can walk with You, talk with You, and run with You through every season.

Your authority never makes our friendship difficult or distant. In fact, it's Your sovereignty that makes it safe for me to be close to You. Because You are in control of all things, I am free to relax, to trust, and to surrender my fears and uncertainties. Your power is not intimidating, but reassuring; Your control does not push me away but draws me in with confidence.

When the journey grows long and the path seems never-ending, I remember that You have already completed the race. You ran the ultimate course through the cross, securing victory, and now You run beside me as I complete my own race. There is never a moment when I run alone.

Because You are the Friend who never leaves my side. You are the steady rhythm guiding each step I take, the quiet voice encouraging me to keep going. Yet, You go even further.

You elevate friendship to a level beyond anything I can imagine by becoming the Helper who dwells within me, bringing Your presence and strength into every part of my life.

7

— • —

HELPER

THE POWER WITHIN

FATHER,

You've shown me so many layers of who You are: Creator, King, Judge, Savior, Father, Friend. I can understand those roles because I've seen them reflected on earth. But You dwelling within me as Helper has no earthly model. No one else can do what You do from within.

"And I will ask the Father, and He will give you another Counselor, to be with you forever. He is the Spirit of truth. The world is unable to receive Him because it doesn't see Him or know Him. But you do know Him, because He remains with you and will be in you" (John 14:16–17).

I've known You as my Helper since I was four years old. That night when I saw my need for a Savior and asked You to save me is the night You came to live within me. In that moment, I experienced the peace of Your presence. It wasn't a feeling or a force. It was You, fully God, choosing to live in me.

You sent Your Spirit to help me relate to You, live for You, and bring others to You.

Help means making it possible or easier for someone to do what they cannot do alone. But help only works when I ask for it. My independent streak resists that. I want to do everything myself, forgetting You designed me for relationship.

You help from above as my Father, beside me as my Friend, and now within me as my Helper. The help You give isn't about taking over. It's about empowering me from within, bridging the gap between my effort and Your divine strength. My work plus Your power equals fruit that glorifies You.

When I write on my own strength, I stare at the blank page, forcing words that don't connect. But when I stop and ask for help, You move through me. Words flow, ideas click, and I see connections I couldn't have seen alone.

When I run on willpower alone, every mile feels like punishment. But when I pray as I run, there's peace under the strain, joy in the movement. You match my pace, strengthening me stride by stride.

That's what You do: You don't remove the work; You make me capable of doing it with purpose and joy.

You teach me empowering dependence so that I learn the paradox of strength through surrender. The more I depend on You, the stronger I become. The more I try to do it alone, the weaker I grow. You empower me not to avoid work but to fulfill it through Your strength.

You haven't changed since Eden. You gave Adam work before sin entered the world. You still call Your children to work, not for salvation or favor, but for Your glory. My work becomes worship when it's done through Your enabling power.

I need help for more than writing and running and working, though. I need help understanding Scripture.

You Help Me Understand and Obey

You illuminate truth and make it alive.

"But the Counselor, the Holy Spirit, whom the Father will send in My name, will teach you all things and remind you of everything I have told you" (John 14:26).

You connect David's fears to my anxieties, Paul's endurance to my calling, Christ's obedience to my daily choices. That's why I can read the same verse a hundred times and see something new each time. You're the Teacher revealing new layers of truth.

And You don't just teach; You help me obey. You cultivate fruit within me that I can't grow on my own, characteristics like love, joy, peace, patience, kindness, goodness, faithfulness, gentleness, and self-control (Galatians 5:22–23). These aren't results of discipline alone. They're evidence of You transforming me from the inside out.

You also keep me on course.

"When He comes, He will convict the world about sin, righteousness, and judgment" (John 16:8).

Your conviction isn't condemnation; it's correction. You don't shame me; You steer me. You convict because You love me too much to let me self-destruct.

You Help Me Overcome and Renew

Temptation never goes away, but You always provide a way through it.

"No temptation has come upon you except what is common to humanity. But God is faithful; He will not allow you to be tempted beyond what you are able, but with the temptation He will also provide a way out so that you may be able to bear it" (1 Corinthians 10:13).

When I rely on You, I can say no to things like sugary sweets that used to master me. As my Helper, You renew my mind daily.

"Do not be conformed to this age, but be transformed by the renewing of your mind, so that you may discern what is the good, pleasing, and perfect will of God" (Romans 12:2).

You've helped me conquer stubborn battles, replacing cravings with discipline, fear with truth, lies with faith. That's renewal in real time, the steady replacement of self-reliance with Spirit-reliance.

This renewal results in peace defies logic.

"Peace I leave with you. My peace I give to you. I do not give to you as the world gives. Don't let your heart be troubled or fearful" (John 14:27).

The world's peace depends on control. Yours comes through surrender. You don't remove storms; You calm hearts within them. When I cast my cares on You, You trade anxiety for assurance. The circumstances may not change, but my perspective does.

Another way You bring peace is by giving me wisdom to navigate a deceptive world.

"Now if any of you lacks wisdom, he should ask of God — who gives to all generously and ungrudgingly — and it will be given to him" (James 1:5).

Wisdom isn't just facts; it's discernment. It's the ability to see truth through fog. You blend insight, experience, and Scripture into clarity I couldn't reach on my own.

When I Resist Your Help

Even knowing this, I resist. I grieve You when I ignore conviction. I quench You when I insist on my own strength. My pride and fear clog the flow of Your Spirit.

It's like building a dam across a river. The water is there, ready to rush through, but I block it with self-reliance. The moment I yield, the river rushes in with power, peace, clarity, and courage, all evidence of Your presence working again.

Whether I'm confessing sin or casting my cares on You, You even help me pray. When words fail, You intercede.

Like when my dad fell after stepping on that rotten deck railing, fracturing his back and ribs. I wasn't sure he was going to survive. I prayed with fervent desperation and urgency unlike I have ever prayed before.

"In the same way, the Spirit also helps us in our weakness, because we do not know what to pray for as we should, but the Spirit himself intercedes for us with unspoken groanings" (Romans 8:26).

My emotions were so overwhelming I struggled to sort them out, much less put them into coherent prayers. In times like those, You take my yearning and present it to the Father with divine eloquence.

I thank You for answering my pleas and healing my dad.

Indwelling and Filling

When I accepted Christ, You sealed me forever. This indwelling marks a permanent relationship, but I have learned that there is a distinct difference between being indwelt by the Spirit and being continually filled with Him.

The Scripture says, "And don't get drunk with wine, which leads to reckless living, but be filled by the Spirit" (Ephesians 5:18). Both experiences — being drunk and being filled — require surrender, but each leads to radically different outcomes. Wine can control and ultimately destroy, while Your Spirit fills and restores. To be filled is to willingly open every part of myself, inviting You to flow through me without resistance.

This surrender is transformative. That is how You take my natural gifts and infuse them with supernatural power.

"Now there are different gifts, but the same Spirit" (1 Corinthians 12:4).

Whether I teach, write, or lead, when I am surrendered to You, You amplify my abilities beyond what I can achieve alone. When I attempt to perform in my own strength, my words and actions fall flat. But when I ask for Your help, my efforts carry weight because they carry You.

Living filled with the Spirit means I speak truth boldly, act with wisdom, and love selflessly. Conversely, when I resist Your filling, I stagnate. The choice is always before me: to control or to surrender, to remain stagnant or to let Your Spirit flow through every aspect of my life.

The Helper Who Holds It All Together

The Helper doesn't just empower me individually; He makes every other relationship with You possible.

Without You, the Helper, I couldn't hear You as my Friend.

Without You, I couldn't trust You as my Father.

Without You, I couldn't obey You as my King or reflect You as my Creator.

Without You, I couldn't stand confident before You as my Judge.

You are the bond between all these roles, the power that turns theology into life. You weave creation, kingship, justice, salvation, fatherhood, and friendship into one living relationship. You make intimacy with God possible, vibrant, and real.

Thank You for being my Helper, the God who transforms me from within.

You never leave, never withdraw, never stop working. Every conviction teaches me. Every correction protects me. Every whisper of guidance draws me closer to You.

I know I will stand before You one day as my Judge, but I can stand without fear because my Savior has already declared me righteous. Still, I long to hear You say, "Well done, good and faithful servant." So help me live aligned with You now.

Your authority as Helper secures me. It means I never face a moment alone. You are the God within — the Counselor, Comforter, and Companion of my every breath.

8

— • —

THE INTEGRATION

LIVING IN RELATIONSHIP WITH THE KING WHO BEFRIENDS

FATHER,

You've shown me layers of who You are and the ways You relate to me. What amazes me most is that You — Father, Son, and Spirit — are all of these roles at once. You don't stop being one to become another. You are always my Creator, always my King, always my Judge, always my Savior, always my Father, always my Friend, and always my Helper.

Because You are all of these roles all at once, I get to have a relationship with You that is both awe-filled and intimate. You are not far away. You are near, known, and present in everything. You reveal Yourself through creation, through Your Word, through Your Spirit, and through the life You breathe into me every day.

Who You Are

You are my Creator. You are the One who imagined me, designed me, and formed me with intention. You gave me life and purpose, making me in Your image to reflect Your glory. Because You created me, You have authority over me.

You are my King. You are the One who rules in righteousness and establishes order. You set boundaries that bring freedom. You govern with wisdom and compassion. You are not a tyrant; You are a protector. Under Your rule, I am safe.

You are my Judge. You the One who upholds truth and evaluates every choice. You see motives, not just actions. You don't judge to condemn but to reveal what's true, calling me to account for what I do with the life You give me.

You are my Savior. Father, You planned my redemption. Christ, You stepped down from the throne, took on flesh, and bore my sin. You took my punishment so I could be free. You bridged the gap I could never cross. Spirit, You applied that salvation when You came to live in me. Because of You — Father, Son, and Spirit — I can stand forgiven. Because of You, I can come home.

You are my Father. Father, You are the One who adopted me. You gave me a new name, a new identity, and a new inheritance. I am Yours. You discipline because You love me, provide because You care, train because You want me to grow, and delight because I am Your child.

You are my Friend. Christ, You are the One who walks beside me. You invite me into conversation, share Your heart, and never leave my side.

You are my Helper. Spirit, You are the One who lives within me. You empower what I cannot do alone. You guide when I'm lost, comfort when I'm hurting, strengthen when I'm weak, and teach when I'm stubborn. You make obedience possible and transformation inevitable.

God, this is why I can have a relationship with You. You are not unreachable. You are here, near, and within. You've made Yourself fully accessible through Christ.

The Christ Bridge

Everyone on earth relates to You as Creator, King, and Judge. That's unavoidable. You made us, You rule us, and You will evaluate us whether we acknowledge it or not. These roles reveal Your absolute authority.

But only believers have the privilege of knowing You as Father, Friend, and Helper, roles reserved for those who belong to Your family.

And Christ as Savior is the bridge between the two.

"Jesus told him, 'I am the way, the truth, and the life. No one comes to the Father except through Me'" (John 14:6).

Every person faces this question: *What will I do with Christ?*

Ignoring or rejecting Him means collision with the Creator, King, and Judge. Accepting Him brings fellowship with the Father, Friend, and Helper.

Without Christ, Your power terrifies. With Him, it comforts. Your authority doesn't change, but Christ changes how I experience it.

"For from Him and through Him and to Him are all things. To him be the glory forever. Amen" (Romans 11:36).

Fighting for What Matters

You didn't save me to live for myself. You rescued me to participate in Your mission to redeem and restore mankind. That means embracing the reality that I'm in a battle, living with eternal urgency, and finishing the work You've given me.

"Fight the good fight of the faith. Take hold of eternal life to which you were called and about which you have made a good confession in the presence of many witnesses" (1 Timothy 6:12).

My flesh craves comfort over calling. The world demands conformity over courage. The enemy whispers lies about my worth. But You call me to fight for what matters eternally.

When I'm tempted to write what sells instead of what serves Your truth, help me fight for integrity. When fear tells me to stay silent, help me speak boldly. When pride tempts me to build my platform over Your kingdom, remind me who I serve.

"Be sober-minded, be alert. Your adversary the devil is prowling around like a roaring lion, looking for anyone he can devour" (1 Peter 5:8).

As my Creator, You equip me. As my Friend, You fight beside me. As my Helper, You strengthen me. As my Judge, You remind me of eternity. As my Father, You bless with me with everything I need for battle. Let me fight knowing the King of the universe and the Savior who defeats of death stands with me.

Living with Eternity in View

Remind me daily that eternity is real, that every soul will spend forever somewhere.

"And they will go away into eternal punishment, but the righteous into eternal life" (Matthew 25:46).

That truth destroys complacency. Every conversation becomes an opportunity to point someone toward You. Every relationship carries eternal weight.

"But in your hearts regard Christ the Lord as holy, ready at any time to give a defense to anyone who asks you for a reason for the hope that is in you" (1 Peter 3:15).

You've placed me where I can make an impact in writing, in running, in family. You've given me a story to tell and a mission to fulfill. Let my life be a beacon that draws others to You. Give me courage to speak and wisdom to know when to listen.

Because You don't just save me *from* hell; You're saving me *to* holiness. You're shaping me into someone who can fully enjoy eternity with You.

"We all, with unveiled faces, are looking as in a mirror at the glory of the Lord and are being transformed into the same image from glory to glory; this is from the Lord who is the Spirit" (2 Corinthians 3:18).

As my Father, You discipline me. As my Friend, You speak truth even when it stings. As my Helper, You convict and cleanse. As my Judge, You remind me what will matter forever.

"Therefore, my dear friends, just as you have always obeyed, so now, not only in my presence but even more in my absence, work out your own salvation with fear and trembling. For it is God who is working in you both to will and to work according to His good purpose" (Philippians 2:12–13).

Strip away pride and fear. Build in me love that reaches beyond comfort, joy that rises above circumstance, and peace that surpasses understanding.

Finishing Strong

I want to finish the work You've given me.

"I glorified You on the earth by completing the work you gave me to do" (John 17:4).

You've entrusted me with stories to write, truths to teach, children to love, and a mission to live. Help me steward every gift faithfully, not for recognition but for Your kingdom impact. Let my discipline and determination serve eternal purposes, not temporary success.

Teach me to live an eternity-focused, character-driven, faithful Christian lifestyle.

"But seek first the kingdom of God and His righteousness, and all these things will be provided for you" (Matthew 6:33).

You are my Creator who made me for Your purpose. My King who rules with wisdom. My Savior who secures my eternity. My Father who provides. My Friend who walks beside me. My Helper who empowers me. My Judge who rewards faithfulness.

Two Different Judgments

One day I will stand before You as my Judge. What I do with Christ while I live determines which judgment I will face: the Great White Throne for unbelievers or the Judgment Seat for believers.

Those who deny Christ in this life will face the Judge at the Great White Throne. The verdict is certain: guilty. The penalty is certain: hell.

No second chances. No appeals. No hope.

As one who trusts Christ, I will not face the verdict that ends in hell.

"Therefore, there is now no condemnation for those in Christ Jesus" (Romans 8:1).

My destiny is secured by blood, not behavior.

Yet I will stand before the Judgment Seat to account for my stewardship as God's child.

"For we must all appear before the judgment seat of Christ, so that each may be repaid for what he has done in the body, whether good or evil" (2 Corinthians 5:10).

On that day, You won't determine where I will spend eternity but reveal how I invested the grace I received. Did I build on Christ with gold, silver, and costly stones, or with wood, hay, and straw? Did I steward what my You entrusted? Did I choose Your glory over my comfort?

This judgment doesn't threaten salvation; it tests faithfulness and determines what rewards I will receive...or lose.

When I stand before You, I want to hear, "Well done, good and faithful servant." Let every conversation, every word, every act of service reflect Your glory.

You are the King who befriends, and I am Your friend who serves the King.

Forever and always.

In Jesus' name,

Amen.

ANSWER THE KING

The Invitation

The King who befriends is standing at the door of your heart and knocking.

He's not waiting to judge you for what you haven't done. He's waiting to walk with you into what He's prepared for you.

Will you open the door?

Will you let the King who befriends become not just your Savior, but your Father, your Friend, your Helper?

Will you stop keeping Him at arm's length and risk the vulnerability of true intimacy?

Will you surrender your independence and discover empowering dependence?

He's already proven His love. He's already paid the price. He's already made the way.

Now He's waiting for your response.

The King of the universe who needs nothing wants you.

The Holy One who cannot tolerate sin calls you friend.

The Judge who has every right to condemn adopts you as His child.

That's the wonder of the King who befriends.

So don't rush past this question: ***What will you do with Christ?***

That single decision determines everything. Will you spend your days here on earth clashing with the Creator/King/Judge and separated from Him for eternity? Or will you spend today and forever in fellowship with the Father/Friend/Helper?

This choice doesn't just shape eternity; it transforms the quality of life here and now. The closer we draw to God, the deeper our peace becomes. Not because life gets easier. We live in a sin-cursed world and will continue to face battles and heartbreak daily. But because God is with us in everything, He gives peace and power that transcends understanding.

What will you do with this truth?

Your next step depends on where you are right now.

If You've Never Accepted Christ

Let's start with the most important question: Have you accepted Christ as your Savior?

Everything in this book hinges on this decision. Without Christ, you remain under the authority of Creator/King/Judge but cut off from the intimacy of Father/Friend/Helper. That's not a threat. It's reality.

The gospel is simple: You're a sinner. God is holy. Your sin separates You from God. You deserve God's wrath. Christ bore God's wrath in your place. "But God proves His own love for us in that while we were still sinners, Christ died for us" (Romans 5:8). Believe in Him and you're saved.

Right now, you can pray something like this:

"God, I am a sinner. I deserve Your judgment. But I believe that Jesus died for my sins and rose from the dead. I believe He is Lord. Save me. Make me Yours. I want to know You as Father, Friend, and Helper, not just as Judge."

If you just prayed that and meant it, welcome to the family. You're forgiven and adopted. Now the journey of knowing God in all His roles begins.

Your next steps:

1. Tell someone about your decision.

2. Find a Bible-believing church to attend and.

3. Start reading the Bible; the Gospel of John is a great place to begin.

Keep talking to God. He's your Father now. Talk to Him like someone who loves you. Because He does.

You don't have to have it all figured out. You just took the most important step. Now walk forward one day at a time.

If You're a Believer but Have Been Distant

Maybe you accepted Christ years ago, but you've been keeping God at a distance. You know Him as Savior so your "ticket to heaven" is secure, but you don't really know Him as Father, Friend, or Helper.

You pray when you're in crisis. You read the Bible occasionally. You show up to church. But there's no daily dependence. No transforming intimacy.

Here's your invitation: *Come back*.

Not to earn His love. You already have it. Not to prove yourself. Christ already did that. But to experience the fullness of relationship He's offering.

Start simple:

- Talk to God every morning before you do anything else.

- Read one chapter of the Bible daily. Ask the Helper to illuminate it as you read.

- Choose one relational role (Father, Friend, or Helper) and focus on experiencing God in that way this month.

The King who befriends is waiting for you with open arms. You already belong to Him. Now learn what it means to walk with Him.

If You're a Believer Pursuing God and Want to Go Deeper

You've been walking with God faithfully. You know Him. You love Him. But you're hungry for more.

This book wasn't meant to give you everything. It was meant to ignite something.

So here's your challenge:

Take one role you struggle to experience and dig deeper. Maybe you intellectually know God as Father, but you don't emotionally feel His love. Maybe you believe He's your Friend but keep Him at arm's length. Maybe you know the Helper lives in you but rarely rely on His empowerment.

Pick one. Spend the next 30 days pursuing God specifically in that role:

- Study every Scripture about that role.

- Ask the Helper to open your eyes to what you're missing.

- Be honest with God about where you're stuck.

Knowing God is a lifelong adventure. You'll never exhaust Him. Every day brings new discovery.

"You will seek Me and find Me when you search for Me with all your heart" (Jeremiah 29:13).

Start Tomorrow Morning

If you're not sure where to begin, here's a simple morning rhythm that integrates all seven roles.

Tomorrow morning, before you do anything else, **spend ninety seconds praying to the Father in the name of the Son through the power of the Spirit** by acknowledging who God is and who you are in Him:

Father,

You exist. You spoke the world into existence. I matter because You made me.

You are my King. You are in charge. You get to make the rules. I am subject to Your authority and surrender to You as Your faithful servant.

I give You my heart, my dreams, my time, my money, my all.

Thank You for holding me accountable to Your standards and for saving me when I could not save myself. I deserved the penalty of eternal damnation.

But Christ bore Your wrath, covered my sin with His blood, and defeated death so I could be adopted into Your family.

I am IN CHRIST! Filled with Your power. Surrounded by Your friendship. Guaranteed an inheritance in Your kingdom.

Now the King who made me, saved me, and adopted me gives me gifts to use, dreams to pursue, and people to love along the way.

Help me use those gifts for Your glory, achieve those dreams with Your assistance, and pour into the lives of my family and friends the way You pour into mine as my Father and Friend.

I don't want to live today in my own strength. So empower me from within. Show Yourself strong through me today.

Help me to live in such a way that at the end of the day, You can say, "Well done, good and faithful servant."

In Christ,

Amen

That's ninety seconds. You can do ninety seconds.

Do this tomorrow, then the next day, then the next. Watch what happens when you start each day acknowledging who God is and who you are in Him.

What I Want You to Know

I'm still learning this.

I wrote this book, but that doesn't mean I've arrived. Some days I experience God as my Friend. Some days I keep Him at arm's length. Some days I depend on my Helper. Some days I exhaust myself trying to do everything alone.

I still struggle with independence. I still forget that my King's rules create freedom. I still pursue my dreams in my power instead of letting Him work through me.

This isn't a book from someone who's mastered relationship with God. It's from someone desperate to know Him more.

So we're in this together. We're both learning to walk with the King who befriends, to surrender to the Helper who empowers, and to grow in understanding who God is.

That's what He wants: not perfection, but pursuit. Not arrival, but hunger. Not self-sufficiency, but empowering dependence.

So let's keep going. Together.

What This Book Can and Can't Do

Before you close this book, understand this:

It **can't** replace actually knowing God. Reading about Him isn't the same as talking to Him.

It **can't** substitute for Scripture. This book points to the Bible, but it's not the Bible.

It **can't** make relationship automatic. Knowing God takes daily, intentional pursuit.

It **can't** answer every question. God is infinite, and this only scratches the surface.

But here's what it **can** do:

- Give you a framework for understanding how God relates to you.

- Point you to the One who wants to be known.

- Show that God's authority and intimacy aren't enemies — they're inseparable.

Now the real work begins: walking daily with the King who befriends.

Make Eternity Your Filter

Live differently because of who He is:

- Let His role as **Creator** remind you that you have purpose.

- Let His role as **King** give you security in His sovereignty.

- Let His role as **Judge** motivate you toward faithfulness.

- Let His role as **Savior** fill you with gratitude and boldness.

- Let His role as **Father** assure you that you're loved unconditionally.

- Let His role as **Friend** invite you into vulnerable intimacy.

- Let His role as **Helper** empower you to do what you cannot do alone.

What dreams is God calling you to pursue for His kingdom? What gifts has He given you to steward for His glory? What people has He placed in your life who need to know Him? What fears or pleasures must you surrender to live boldly for Him?

Every day matters. Every choice counts. Every conversation is an opportunity to reflect the King who befriends.

Don't waste your life on anything smaller than His eternal purposes.

Now go walk with Him and let the world see His friendship through you.

ACKNOWLEDGEMENTS

To My Trusted Reviewers:

My Parents, Harry and Janice Schaefer: Thank you for leading me to Christ, modeling what a close relationship with Him looks like, and reviewing this manuscript to ensure theological accuracy.

My Pastor John Holmes: Thank you for taking the time to review this manuscript and provide feedback. Your commitment to sound doctrine and your pastoral heart have been invaluable in ensuring this book reveals how God's authority enables intimate relationship rather than preventing it.

To the Teachers Who Help Me Know God More Deeply: Alistair Begg (*Truth For Life*), Tony Evans (*The Urban Alternative*), and Chip Ingram (*Living on the Edge*) — Thank you for fulfilling your ministries. You don't know me, but I listen to you and read your books. Your faithful teaching of God's Word has deepened my understanding of who God is and how He relates to His people. I commend your books and ministries to any reader hungry to grow in their knowledge of God.

ABOUT THE AUTHOR

BONNIE JEAN SCHAEFER IS the Adventurous Author who adventurizes life.

She's on a mission to anchor Christians in who God is so they know who they are — and then live boldly from that place. Her framework? **Start with WHO. And WHO starts with God.**

A lifelong Christian with a Bible degree from Cedarville College (now Cedarville University), Bonnie hosts *The Adventurous Author* podcast and founded Dream Doers Publishing. She writes under her own name for faith and writing content and as D.K. Drake for the *Dragon Stalker Bloodlines* fantasy saga.

The same woman who's crossed five marathon finish lines and tackled 50K trail races approaches faith with equal intensity. She lives in North Carolina with her two sisters, raising four adopted children and proving that anchored people live adventurously as Dream Doers.

The 50 by 50 Mission

Bonnie is publishing 50 books by her 50th birthday. The mission started on her 48th birthday to challenge her to finish books in various stages of the writing process: *The Faithful Christian Living Experience* (12 foundational books), *The Wealthy Writer Experience* (training for God's creatives), and 35+ children's stories through the *Everrlyn Experience* and *Zella Zeal Experience*.

This is book 2 of 50.

Join the adventure at TheAdventurousAuthor.com/league for monthly storytelling tournaments, weekly sparks, and the digital version of every book as it releases — just $7/month.

What adventure is God prompting YOU to start? *And when will you begin?*

— • —

WHY THIS SERIES EXISTS

THE FAITHFUL CHRISTIAN LIVING EXPERIENCE

DEAR READER,

I am not writing these books because I have all the answers. I'm writing them because I have all the questions.

I wanted answers to my questions, so I studied Bible in college and kept digging long after I earned that degree. I gained solid theological knowledge. But knowledge alone wasn't enough.

I could live it with quiet conviction, but I couldn't synthesize it. I couldn't articulate it with clarity. And I didn't have the boldness to speak up and speak out in a way God was calling me to.

So a few years ago, I wanted to distill everything I'd learned from Scripture into a framework that felt like a story rather than systematic theology — a framework I could actually live and speak from, not just study. I wanted to connect the dots in a way that anchored my soul, fueled my faith, and helped me related to my God effectively.

So I started pray-thinking in my journal, wrestling with the foundational questions every Christian needs to answer:

- **Who is God?** What is He like? What makes Him unique?

- **Who is God in relation to me?** Is He distant? Engaged? What does it mean that He calls Himself Creator, King, Judge, Savior, Father, Friend, and Helper?

- **What does God want, and why?** What are His driving purposes, and how does He accomplish them?

- **Why should I trust the Bible?** What makes it different from every other religious text? In a world of noise and deception, how do I know what's real?

- **What happens after I die?** Is eternity real or just a comforting story?

- **Who is Satan?** What does my greatest enemy want, and how does he try to get it?

- **Why do I matter?** What's my purpose in God's eternal plan?

- **How did God design me?** What does it mean to be made in His image — heart, mind, body, and soul?

- **How do I live from this foundation?** What values guide me? What's my character foundation? How do I set goals that honor God?

The Faithful Christian Living Experience books are the result of that wrestling. They are designed to give you a framework for knowing God, understanding yourself, and living faithfully in a world that's hostile to truth.

These 11 catalyst books are designed to anchor your faith:

- **Anchored Faith** (Books 1-3) — Know God, Trust God, Walk with God

- **Anchored Truth** (Books 4-6) — Explore why the Bible is true, the reality of eternity, and your invisible enemy (and how to fight him effectively)

- **Anchored Identity** (Books 7-8) — Discover who you are in Christ and why you are significant

- **Anchored Living** (Books 9-11) — Walk out what you've learned in a way that aligns with God and your design

These aren't theology textbooks. They're conversations with God about identity: His, mine, and yours. Each book builds on the foundation laid before it, because you can't discern truth without first knowing God. You know who you are without building on TRUTH. You can't live effectively without knowing who you are IN CHRIST.

This is the hard work of building unshakeable faith that withstands storms, resists deception, and finishes what God starts.

You'll never reach the end of knowing God. He's infinite, and you're finite. But that's makes seeking Him a thrilling adventure — one that carries through from this life into eternity.

And you don't have to walk this journey alone.

In Christ,

Bonnie Jean Schaefer

P.S. I'd love to hear how this book has impacted your relationship with God. Please share your story as an email to me (bonnie@adventur izelife.com) or as a review on Amazon.

Join the Adventure at TheAdventuruousAuthor.com.

The League of Adventurous Authors

For years, I called myself an "aspiring writer." I had the calling. I had the faith. I had stories burning in my bones.

But I couldn't finish anything.

Random writing bursts. Broken promises. Guilt every time I chose writing over family time. The loop of starting projects and abandoning them at Chapter 3.

That's why I built **The League of Adventurous Authors™**—because I needed the flexible lifestyle system rooted in Christ I couldn't find anywhere else.

It's a Christ-anchored training league that fixes **Creative Identity first** (just like this book anchored you in who God is and who you are in Him), then builds the rhythm that actually lasts.

If you're a Christian fiction author ready to:
- Stop calling yourself "aspiring"
- Write consistently without guilt
- Finish stories you start
- Train for faithfulness, not fame
- ENJOY the process of doing hard things...

Join me in The League at TheAdventurousAuthor.com/league or listen to The Adventurous Author podcast.

Let's train together.

—Bonnie Jean

www.ingramcontent.com/pod-product-compliance
Lightning Source LLC
Chambersburg PA
CBHW031633040426
42452CB00007B/801